TOOLS FOR CAREGIVERS

- **ATOS:** 0.8
- **GRL:** C
- **WORD COUNT:** 21

- **CURRICULUM CONNECTIONS:** animals, habitats

Skills to Teach

- **HIGH-FREQUENCY WORDS:** are, have, these, they, what
- **CONTENT WORDS:** babies, cubs, learn, lion, play, roar, sleep, spots
- **PUNCTUATION:** exclamation point, periods, question mark
- **WORD STUDY:** long /a/, spelled ay (play); long /e/, spelled ee (sleep); long /o/, spelled oa (roar); r-controlled vowels (learn)
- **TEXT TYPE:** information report

Before Reading Activities

- Read the title and give a simple statement of the main idea.
- Have students "walk" though the book and talk about what they see in the pictures.
- Introduce new vocabulary by having students predict the first letter and locate the word in the text.
- Discuss any unfamiliar concepts that are in the text.

After Reading Activities

The last spread of the book mentions that lion cubs roar. Ask the readers to roar like a lion. Why do they think lions roar? Explain that lions communicate through roars. It tells other lions where they are. Or it tells some lions to stay away from their territory. Ask the readers: What other animals roar? Why? How do they think animals use sounds to communicate?

Tadpole Books are published by Jump!, 5357 Penn Avenue South, Minneapolis, MN 55419, www.jumplibrary.com

Copyright ©2019 Jump. International copyright reserved in all countries. No part of this book may be reproduced in any form without written permission from the publisher.

Editor: Jenna Trnka **Designer:** Anna Peterson

Photo Credits: Eric Isselee/Shutterstock, cover, 1, 6–7, 16br; Anup Shah/Age Fotostock, 2–3; dean bertoncelj/Shutterstock, 4–5, 16tl; Nilesh Rathod/iStock, 8–9, 16tr; Guido Bissattini/Shutterstock, 10–11, 16bm; Pranav Chadha/Shutterstock, 12–13, 16tm; Russell Burden/Getty, 14–15, 16bl.

Library of Congress Cataloging-in-Publication Data
Names: Nilsen, Genevieve, author.
Title: Lion cubs / by Genevieve Nilsen.
Description: Tadpole edition. | Minneapolis, MN : Jump!, Inc., (2019) | Series: Safari babies | Includes index.
Identifiers: LCCN 2018024755 (print) | LCCN 2018027524 (ebook) | ISBN 9781641282451 (ebook) | ISBN 9781641282437 (hardcover : alk. paper) | ISBN 9781641282444 (paperback)
Subjects: LCSH: Lion—Infancy—Juvenile literature.
Classification: LCC QL737.C23 (ebook) | LCC QL737.C23 N56 2019 (print) | DDC 599.75713/92—dc23
LC record available at https://lccn.loc.gov/2018024755

SAFARI BABIES

LION CUBS

by Genevieve Nilsen

Summit Free Public Library

TABLE OF CONTENTS

tadpole
books

LION CUBS

What are these babies?

cub ┈┈▶

They are lion cubs.

spots ·····

They have spots.

They play.

They sleep.

They learn.

They roar!

WORDS TO KNOW

cubs   learn   play

roar   sleep   spots

INDEX